the
mediterranean
diet

**Quick and Easy
5-Ingredient Cookbook**

Eat Like the Romans

(AND THE GREEKS AND THE SPANIARDS AND...YOU GET THE IDEA)

START YOUR JOURNEY to a healthier life with a culinary tradition thousands of years in the making: the Mediterranean diet. This book features more than 70 wholesome, delicious dishes, each using five ingredients or less. Read on and discover how you can lose weight, lower your cholesterol, possibly help save the planet and more through this time-tested, heart-healthy diet. What are you waiting for? Let's go to Tuscany!

A Beginner's Guide
TO THE MEDITERRANEAN DIET

Everything you wanted to know about one of the planet's most nutritious meal plans without having to book a flight to Mykonos (but you still should—it's beautiful).

LET'S START WITH WHAT WE KNOW: For reasons that are entirely your own, you want to get started with the Mediterranean diet. Maybe you heard about it from a friend, or perhaps you read an article declaring its benefits and your interest was piqued. It's possible your cardiologist recommended you make some changes in your meal planning and this diet was the first she suggested, or maybe someone gave this book to you as a gift and you know nothing about diets or the Mediterranean or even cooking for yourself. No matter your reasoning for wanting to get started, the good news is you're in good hands. The better news? The Mediterranean diet might be the easiest, healthiest and most flavorful option for anyone looking to change their approach to food. So how do you get started? Well, that's entirely up to you. If you're sold on the efficacy of this diet, then by all means jump right in to the recipe section and you'll start seeing results approximately 10 minutes faster than the folks who choose to read the rest of this introduction. For those of you who have 10 minutes to spare, what follows is a short explanation of the diet's origins, its benefits, its components and a few tips to keep you on track.

WHAT IS THE MEDITERRANEAN DIET?

FOR THOUSANDS OF YEARS, the Mediterranean diet has been a way of life for millions of people. According to the United National Educational, Scientific and Cultural Organization, this particular diet is a composite of cultural dietary traditions from numerous countries, including Cyprus, Croatia, Spain, Greece, Italy, Morocco and Portugal. Its basic principles—eating healthy fats, fruits and vegetables while limiting red meat, cheese and salt—have contributed to historically low rates of heart disease for the people within these communities.

Unlike other diets—such as Atkins, Weight Watchers or keto—the Mediterranean diet wasn't designed by a team of doctors or invented through clinical trials (not that there's anything wrong with that). Amazingly, people adopted this lifestyle organically over time to make the most of their natural resources. It's even protected as an asset of "Intangible Cultural Heritage" by UNESCO. Its anecdotal health benefits were serious enough to demand scientific study, though, which is how the Mediterranean diet first became a topic of dietary discussion. In the 1960s, scientists discovered people who followed this diet had fewer deaths from heart disease than everyone else in the United States and northern Europe.

Today, this largely plant-based approach to eating has received some solid accolades: It's been endorsed as a heart-healthy diet by the Mayo Clinic, lauded as a "healthy and sustainable dietary pattern" by the World Health Organization and even recommended by the Dietary Guidelines for Americans. If that weren't enough to sell you on its merits, the legacy of this diet means you'll be learning healthy recipes that have been passed down through generations—a culinary heritage that can only be described as undeniably delicious.

In the age of the ancient Greeks (and later, the Romans), fashionable people in the region preferred eating seafood to red meat. And with a sea as bountiful as the Mediterranean, who could blame them? Poorer people didn't have the money for meat and took what they could get in the way of bread, olives, vegetables and the occasional salted fish. With the rise and clash of different empires, these basic traditions merged with those of the Arab world, who we can thank for many of the spices we know and love today. The Mediterranean diet reflects the collected culinary wisdom of this region. It embraces foods like olive oil, fish and beans as timeless, healthy resources. In short, it's worked for millions of people for thousands of years. Odds are it'll work for you too.

GOOD FOR YOU, GOOD FOR THE PLANET

YOU MIGHT BE THINKING, "OK, this diet isn't a fad—it's older than the United States." And you're right. But that doesn't mean it's not a

great fit for today's modern world. While vegetarian and vegan diets eliminate meat and other animal products, the Mediterranean diet takes the middle ground, promoting a zen-like balance of all food groups. You can eat red meat occasionally, along with cheese, eggs and yogurt. Where other diets militantly make you cut out carbs or booze, Mediterranean dieters can still have a pasta dinner and kick back with a glass of vino. Engaging with this diet means you don't have to sacrifice any one beloved food from your diet (except for fried chicken, but it's for the best and you knew it was coming).

In a mostly plant-based diet, fruits and vegetables take center stage. The Mediterranean diet does not require large amounts of meat, or any meat at all, if you'd prefer. When you limit the demand for meat, you spare not only animals but the natural resources used to raise livestock, which in turn cuts down on greenhouse gasses. In sum, your decision to go on this diet could help save the planet!

Aside from helping Mother Nature and reconnecting you with ancient traditions, the Mediterranean diet can also improve your quality of life. When you reduce your meat intake, amp up the fruits and veggies and stick to olive oil, you can lower your cholesterol, lose weight and reduce your risk of stroke, diabetes, dementia, breast cancer and even depression. These benefits are not exclusive to the Mediterranean diet, but you'll be hard-pressed to find another program that promises all of them and still produces food you'll enjoy eating.

5 MEDITERRANEAN DIET MYTHS BUSTED

Just a few of the common misconceptions that might hinder your success.

MYTH: THERE IS ONLY ONE MEDITERRANEAN DIET.

Contrary to popular belief, there is no one true Mediterranean diet. Instead, this particular diet keeps things interesting by drawing from several cultures: Greek, Spanish and Italian, among others. This variety means the Mediterranean diet can be easily customized to fit your style and taste while ensuring what are largely the same lasting, life-changing health benefits.

MYTH: THE MEDITERRANEAN DIET IS STRICTLY VEGETARIAN.

As with vegetarian diets, the Mediterranean diet is noteworthy for its emphasis on fruits, vegetables and nuts. However, by no means does the Mediterranean diet eliminate meat or animal products. Poultry and seafood are encouraged, while dairy and red meat are permitted in lean, limited quantities.

MYTH: THE MEDITERRANEAN DIET ALLOWS FOR UNLIMITED PASTA.

If only that were true. While pasta is allowed, it's certainly not encouraged in large—let alone unlimited—portions. You'll have a tough time finding any health-conscious diet which calls for

lots of pasta. But you'd also have difficulty finding a fad diet that makes space for you to enjoy a delicious pasta dish just for the pleasure of it.

MYTH: PEOPLE IN MEDITERRANEAN COUNTRIES EAT LIKE THIS EVERY DAY.

The Mediterranean diet is a reflection of traditional cultural meals—beloved family recipes and styles of cooking that have been passed down from generation to generation. Think of what grandmothers taught their grandchildren to make over a stove at big family occasions. It's more of a collection of delicious memories. Sadly, it's no longer what a majority of Spaniards, Italians, Greeks or others eat every day. The rising popularity of processed and fast foods—both in these countries and around the world—underscores a growing need to maintain a balanced diet in order to prevent obesity and heart disease.

MYTH: THE MEDITERRANEAN DIET ONLY APPLIES TO FOOD.

Actually, this diet promotes several happy lifestyle changes. Food is just one piece of the puzzle. In the Mediterranean region, people make a point of eating with friends and family. Dishes are made with fresh, local ingredients and people prefer to eat slowly, taking the time to savor their food. Portions tend to be small rather than large, and there's an overall cultural preference to spend time outdoors rather than cooped up in the office. Fewer people have

cars, meaning they have to carry groceries on foot by walking or using public transportation. Traditionally speaking, and especially in rural areas today, people buy ingredients from farmers markets every other day rather than shop at chain supermarkets for a week's worth of food. The vegetables are fresh, the fruit is crisp and the attentiveness to what's going to make up your plate each night is part of the lifestyle.

If this particular approach to eating sounds worlds away from American grab-and-go dining, processed foods and meals scarfed down behind desks, that's because it is. It's a much more intimate, intentional way not only to eat but to live. What's not to love? With the Mediterranean diet, you can make simple meals with wholesome ingredients, lose weight and experience a whole-new quality of life you never considered possible outside of sun-drenched Tuscan villas.

HOW TO GET STARTED

Follow these tips to get ready for your
heart-healthy journey with the Mediterranean diet.

EAT SEVEN TO 10 SERVINGS OF FRUITS AND VEGETABLES DAILY.

As a plant-based diet, the Mediterrean diet means learning to love your fruits and veggies. According to the Centers for Disease Control and Prevention, only 1 in 10 adults get their recommended daily intake of fruits and vegetables, which means most people are missing out on crucial vitamins and minerals every day. Eating plenty of fiber-rich foods will help your body stabilize your blood sugar, regulate your bowel movements and make you feel fuller longer—key ingredients to weight loss. You'll be wearing your favorite vintage jeans in no time. Not sure how to start? Try adding half an avocado and place on whole grain toast for a potassium-packed, fiber-filled breakfast you can brag about on Instagram.

EAT FISH TWICE A WEEK—GRILLED OR BAKED, NOT DEEP FRIED.

Fatty fish might be full of omega-3s but you remove a lot of that wholesome natural goodness when you fry your food. Fried foods also have high levels of trans fats, otherwise known as "bad" fats, which lead to high cholesterol, high blood pressure and everything the Mediterranean diet

works to fix. Don't get bitter over batter, though: Grilled fish is both nutritious and delicious.

And, just like your mother always told you, there are plenty of fish in the sea, including tuna, salmon, mackerel, herring, cod, trout and anchovies. Baking your fish is another heart-healthy way to enjoy its protein-packed flavor.

AVOID RED MEAT—USE FISH, POULTRY OR BEANS INSTEAD.

It's no secret Americans eat a lot of meat. In 2018, The U.S. Department of Agriculture estimated the average American would consume 222 pounds of meat that year alone. That's the equivalent of eating two-and-a-half burgers every day. There's also bad news for all you bacon lovers: The World Health Organization classifies processed meat as "carcinogenic" because it's been linked to cancer. The good news: You can lower your cholesterol and saturated fat intake by sticking to fish, chicken and beans. If you do decide to eat red meat (and who can deny a good steak every now and then?), keep portions small and lean.

INCORPORATE WHOLE GRAINS.

Though it might make for yummy peanut butter and jelly sandwiches, white bread is low in

nutrients and high in calories and carbs. On its own, white bread doesn't give you much protein or fiber. Amp up that PB&J (or any other sandwich) by switching to whole-grain bread, which has higher amounts of crucial vitamins and minerals, including manganese and selenium, that reduce inflammation.

USE HEALTHY FATS.

Healthy fats may sound like an oxymoron, but not only are they real, they can add serious flavor to your cooking routine too. Also known as "good" fats, monounsaturated and polyunsaturated fats will lower your risk of heart disease and stroke as well as prevent inflammation. You can find these in foods like avocados, olives, nuts, peanut butter, tofu and fatty fish (think salmon or tuna). Replace your usual butter or margarine with olive oil when cooking, or feel free to switch it up and use sesame oil. Worried about missing out on dessert? Don't sweat it: You can always treat yourself to some divine dark chocolate.

SKIP THE SALT.

Step away from the shaker! A diet heavy in salt can lead to bloating, weight gain and high blood pressure, the last of which the American Heart Association calls a "silent killer" because the symptoms aren't always obvious. Nine in 10 people are expected to develop high blood pressure throughout their lives, which means there's a huge downside to being salty. How do you add flavor without increasing your risk of heart disease? Get creative with herbs and spices like rosemary, thyme,

oregano, cinnamon and paprika. Your house will smell amazing and your heart will thank you.

EAT DAIRY IN MODERATION.

Let's face it: A bit of ice cream is good for the soul. There's nothing wrong with the occasional creamy treat. For protein-packed options, opt for low-fat Greek or plain yogurt. You can also eat cheese—just be sure to vary it up and keep portions small. Definitely don't bust out the old fondue set just yet, but you can sneak a slice of brie every now and then.

TAKE A WALK.

All of the health benefits of the Mediterranean diet come together when you add aerobic exercise to the mix. Whether you run, walk, hike, swim or more, 30 minutes to an hour of exercise a day will help you in your weight loss journey and keep your heart healthy and strong.

To eat well is to live well! You can lower your cholesterol, reduce your risk of chronic disease, fight climate change and more by engaging with the Mediterranean diet. All it takes is making a few easy changes to your favorite meals. Rediscover your love of food (and keep the weight off) with these wholesome, time-tested recipes you can start cooking today. Saving the planet and yourself never tasted so good.

So what are you waiting for? Read on and enjoy more than 70 delicious recipes that are all Mediterranean diet–approved.

Breakfast

START YOUR DAY WITH ANY
OF THESE DELICIOUS
MORNING MEALS.

ROASTED EGGPLANT AND EGGS

INGREDIENTS
1 large eggplant
¼ cup salt
2 cups Marinara sauce (your favorite)
4 slices mozzarella cheese
8 eggs, poached

DIRECTIONS
Preheat oven to 350 degrees F.

Slice the eggplants into ½-inch rounds, making eight slices. Place the eggplant rounds in a colander and sprinkle with salt. Let the eggplant drain for about 30 minutes to 1 hour. Whip off the salt and set on a parchment-lined baking sheet. Cook the eggplant in a preheated oven for about 10 to 15 minutes, or until softened.

Warm the sauce in a medium saucepan over medium-low heat. Place an even amount of sauce onto each eggplant and a slice of cheese on each. Top the eggplants with a poached egg and serve.

SERVES 4

PER SERVING
Calories: 338.9 | Total Fat: 19.1g | Saturated Fat: 7.2g | Cholesterol: 444.4mg | Sodium: 490.9mg | Potassium: 820.6mg | Total Carbohydrates: 20g | Dietary Fiber: 5.4g | Sugars: 11.6g | Protein: 22g

Tomato and Egg
BREAKFAST BAKE

INGREDIENTS

1½ pints grape tomatoes (multi-colored, if available)
1 small red onion, sliced thin
1 tsp red pepper flakes
4 large eggs
¼ cup feta cheese

DIRECTIONS

Preheat oven to 375 degrees F.

Place the tomatoes, onions and red pepper flakes into an oven-safe nonstick baking dish. Place the baking dish into the preheated oven and cook for 10 minutes, or until the tomatoes are softened.

Crack the eggs on top of the cooked tomatoes and return to the oven. Cook for 5 minutes, or until the eggs are set and the yolk is still runny. Take out of the oven and sprinkle with feta cheese and serve.

SERVES 4

PER SERVING
Calories: 137.6 | Total Fat: 8.9g | Saturated Fat: 3.4g | Cholesterol: 192.3mg | Sodium: 200.2mg | Potassium: 112.3mg | Total Carbohydrates: 5.5g | Dietary Fiber: 0.9g | Sugars: 3.3g | Protein: 8.4g

PITA BREAD POCKETS

INGREDIENTS

8 eggs
1 Tbsp olive oil
2 tsp capers
2 small ripe tomatoes, diced
4 whole-grain pita bread pockets

DIRECTIONS

In a large nonstick pan with olive oil, cook the eggs on medium-low heat, stirring frequently with a rubber spatula, until the eggs are cooked but still moist.

Fill each pita bread with the capers, tomatoes and cooked eggs. Serve.

SERVES 4

Season with salt and pepper if desired

PER SERVING
Calories: 388.2 | Total Fat: 18.5g | Saturated Fat: 4.7g | Cholesterol: 338mg | Sodium: 592mg | Potassium: 293mg | Total Carbohydrates: 37.7g | Dietary Fiber: 4.8g | Sugars: 3.5g | Protein: 18.6g

Greek Yogurt
BREAKFAST BOWL

INGREDIENTS

4 cups full-fat Greek yogurt
1 Tbsp vanilla
4 Tbsp honey
½ cup crushed almonds
2 cups quartered figs

DIRECTIONS

Stir the vanilla into the yogurt. Place a cup of yogurt into four serving bowls, top each evenly with honey, almonds and figs, then serve.

SERVES 4

PER SERVING
Calories 416.5 | Total Fat: 19.9g | Saturated Fat: 9.5g | Cholesterol: 50mg | Sodium: 151.1mg | Total Carbohydrates: 48.3g | Dietary Fiber: 4g | Sugars: 43.2g | Protein: 12.1g

Morning
EGG OMELET ROLL

INGREDIENTS

8 eggs
1 Tbsp olive oil
2 avocados, thinly sliced
3 tomatoes, chopped
⅓ lb lox (smoked salmon),
**   broken into small pieces**

DIRECTIONS

Preheat oven to
350 degrees F.

In a large bowl, whisk
together the eggs. Brush
a 14½-by-9½-inch baking
sheet with olive oil, line
the greased baking sheet
with parchment paper
and grease the parchment
paper. Pour the eggs onto
the baking sheet and cook
in a preheated oven for
10 minutes, or until the
eggs are set.

Place the avocados (saving
4 slices for presentation),
tomatoes (saving ½ cup
for presentation) and lox
evenly on top of the cooked
eggs. Roll the egg, jelly
roll–style, widthwise, cut
into four equal-size rolls.
Garnish the top of each
roll with the remaining
avocados and tomatoes.
Serve.

SERVES 4

*Can be served with toast
*Season with salt and
pepper if desired

PER SERVING
Calories: 389.3 | Total Fat: 28.6g |
Saturated Fat: 6.2g | Cholesterol:
385.3mg | Sodium: 528.1mg |
Total Carbohydrates: 12.6g |
Dietary Fiber: 6.9g | Sugars: 0.6g |
Protein: 24.4g

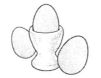

Spanakopita
CREPES

IINGREDIENTS
1 onion, diced
2 Tbsp olive oil
3 cups fresh spinach
½ cup crumbled feta cheese
8 whole-grain crepes (store-bought or homemade)

DIRECTIONS
In a large nonstick skillet with oil over medium heat, cook the onions until tender and translucent, about 3 to 4 minutes. Add in the spinach, continue to cook, stirring often, until the spinach is heated through. Stir in the feta cheese.

Warm or cook the crepes. Evenly stuff each crepe with filling and serve.

SERVES 4

PER SERVING
Calories: 643 | Total Fat: 16.9g | Saturated Fat: 5.5g | Cholesterol: 230.7mg | Sodium: 409.6mg | Potassium: 164.7mg | Total Carbohydrates: 93.9g | Dietary Fiber: 3.2g | Sugars: 21.2g | Protein: 27.1g

Almond
FRENCH TOAST BAKE

INGREDIENTS
12 slices whole-wheat bread
12 eggs
1 tsp vanilla
½ cup almond butter
1 cup crushed almonds

DIRECTIONS
Preheat oven to 375 degrees F.

Cut all crust off the bread and tear into small pieces. Place the bread in an oven-safe baking dish sprayed with cooking spray.

In a large bowl, whisk the eggs, add the vanilla and almond butter and whisk to combine. Pour the egg mixture over the bread and let it absorb the egg mixture. Top with crushed almonds, cover with foil and bake in the preheated oven for about 30 minutes. Remove the foil and cook for another 10 minutes, or until the top is lightly browned. Serve.

SERVES 4

PER SERVING
Calories: 753.3 | Total Fat: 46.8g | Saturated Fat: 7.6g | Cholesterol: 558mg | Sodium: 513.8mg | Potassium 791.9mg | Total Carbohydrates: 46.9g | Dietary Fiber: 11.8g | Sugars 8.1g | Protein 39.1g

Very Berry DUTCH BABIES

INGREDIENTS
3 eggs
⅔ cup almond milk
¾ cup white whole-wheat flour
¼ tsp vanilla extract
3 cups mixed berries (your favorites)

DIRECTIONS
Preheat oven to 425 degrees F. Place four hot individual-serving cast-iron skillets or one large hot skillet into the oven.

In a large bowl, whisk the eggs until well combined, add the milk, flour and vanilla, and stir until just combined. Spray the skillets with cooking spray and then add the batter. The batter should bubble at the edges. Place in the oven and cook for about 20 minutes, or until light and fluffy.

Top each evenly with assorted berries and serve.

SERVES 4

Can be served with syrup or honey if desired

PER SERVING
Calories: 181 | Total Fat: 4.8g | Saturated Fat: 1.2g | Cholesterol: 139.5mg | Sodium: 82.2mg | Potassium: 220.4mg | Total Carbohydrates: 25.2g | Dietary Fiber: 6.2g | Sugars: 0.2g | Protein: 10.1g

Lemon Ricotta PANCAKES

INGREDIENTS

3 eggs
1 cup ricotta cheese
1 cup white whole-wheat flour
1 cup almond milk
1 lemon, juice and zest

DIRECTIONS

Separate the eggs. Take the egg whites and whip with a hand blender until white peaks form.

Place ricotta in a blender and blend until smooth.

In a large bowl, add the blended ricotta, egg yolks, flour, milk and lemon juice and zest. Stir to combine. Fold in the egg whites until just combined.

In a nonstick pan, cook the pancakes on each side until lightly browned and cooked through. Serve.

SERVES 4

PER SERVING
Calories: 273.9 | Total Fat: 12.8g | Saturated Fat: 6.3g | Cholesterol: 170.9mg | Sodium: 148.2mg | Potassium: 195.5mg | Total Carbohydrates: 23.3g | Dietary Fiber: 4.5g | Sugars: 0.3g | Protein: 16.2g

Vegetable
WAFFLE OMELETS

INGREDIENTS
8 eggs
½ red pepper, diced
½ cup mushrooms
1 small onion, diced
2 Tbsp olive oil

DIRECTIONS
Beat the eggs in a medium bowl.

In a medium pan, with 1 tablespoon olive oil over medium heat, cook the peppers, mushrooms and onions until softened, about 4 to 5 minutes. Let cool.

Add the vegetable mixture into the eggs.

Preheat a waffle iron. Brush the waffle iron with oil and place eggs ¼ to ½ cup at a time, depending on the size of your waffle iron. Cook until the eggs are cooked through and serve.

SERVES 4

PER SERVING
Calories: 255.3 | Total Fat: 20.2g | Saturated Fat: 4.9g | Cholesterol: 338mg | Sodium: 177.2mg | Potassium: 249.9mg | Total Carbohydrates: 5g | Dietary Fiber: 0.8g | Sugars: 3.4g | Protein: 12.8g

Banana
PANCAKES

INGREDIENTS
4 ripe bananas
3 eggs
½ cup almond butter
½ Tbsp cinnamon
2 Tbsp olive oil

DIRECTIONS
Combine all ingredients (except olive oil) in a blender and blend until smooth.

In a nonstick pan, with olive oil over medium heat, cook the pancakes about 2 minutes on each side, or until the pancakes rise, slightly brown and cook through. Serve.

SERVES 4

PER SERVING
Calories 381.9 | Total Fat: 28.1g | Saturated Fat: 3.6g | Cholesterol: 139.5mg | Sodium: 58.3mg | Potassium: 587.1mg | Total Carbohydrates: 26.8g | Dietary Fiber: 6.2g | Sugars: 11.5g | Protein: 10.3g

White Bean
TOASTS

INGREDIENTS
4 slices whole-grain bread
2 cups white beans
16 stalks asparagus
4 hard-boiled eggs, sliced
⅓ cup tahini

DIRECTIONS
Place the bread on a hot grill or in a toaster and toast on both sides until golden brown and crispy.

Place the asparagus onto a hot grill and grill on all sides until tender, about 3 to 4 minutes.

Place the beans in a bowl and smash with a fork until you achieve a chunky texture.

Place an even amount of white beans onto the toasted bread, then top evenly with the asparagus and eggs. Drizzle each with an equal amount of tahini and serve.

SERVES 4

Season with salt and pepper if desired

PER SERVING
Calories: 462.8 | Total Fat: 19.2g | Saturated Fat: 4.2g | Cholesterol: 253mg | Sodium: 302.6mg | Potassium: 779.9mg | Total Carbohydrates: 52.9g | Dietary Fiber: 11.2g | Sugars: 1.4g | Protein: 26.4g

Breakfast
FLATBREADS

INGREDIENTS
4 whole-grain flatbreads
1 cup chickpeas
2 avocados, sliced
4 hard-boiled eggs, chopped
4 Tbsp chili-flavored olive oil

DIRECTIONS
Preheat oven or grill to 350 degrees F.

Place the flatbreads on a baking sheet or grill and toast until golden brown. Remove from heat and evenly top each with the chickpeas, avocados and eggs. Drizzle each with the flavored oil and serve.

SERVES 4

PER SERVING
Calories: 451.7 | Total Fat: 28.6g | Saturated Fat: 4.5g | Cholesterol: 253mg | Sodium: 460.5mg | Potassium: 627.4mg | Total Carbohydrates: 33.9g | Dietary Fiber: 11.5g | Sugars: 3g | Protein: 17.2g

Breakfast
PANINI

INGREDIENTS

8 slices sugar-free, whole-grain bread
½ cup hummus
4 hard-boiled eggs, sliced
2 cups fresh spinach
4 slices mozzarella cheese

DIRECTIONS

Preheat waffle iron or pan.

Place four slices of bread down on a prep area. Spread each slice evenly with hummus, top each with an egg, an even amount of spinach and mozzarella cheese. Top each with the remaining bread and toast each with a waffle iron or pan until the cheese has melted. Serve.

SERVES 4

PER SERVING
Calories: 532.5 | Total Fat: 26.8g | Saturated Fat: 9.5g | Cholesterol: 528.3mg | Sodium: 856.7mg | Potassium: 347.9mg | Total Carbohydrates: 45.3g | Dietary Fiber: 8.2g | Sugars: 1.9g | Protein: 36.3

Baked
OATMEAL APPLES

INGREDIENTS
4 large honey crisp apples
2 cups old-fashioned oats
½ cup chopped dates
2 Tbsp cinnamon
2 cups almond milk

DIRECTIONS
Preheat oven to 400 degrees F.

Thoroughly wash the apples. Core the apples by cutting around the core with a knife or apple corer from the top and lifting out the core and seeds. Leave the bottom intact so it can be stuffed.

Hollow out the apple, leaving ¼ inch of the outer edge. Chop the apple pieces that have been removed.

In a medium bowl, mix together the chopped apples, oats, dates and cinnamon. Stuff each apple with mixture and pour almond milk into each apple.

Place the stuffed apples in an oven-safe baking dish and place in the preheated oven. Bake for about 40 minutes, or until the oatmeal and apple are softened. Add more almond milk during cooking if the oatmeal seems dry. Remove from the oven and serve.

SERVES 4

PER SERVING
Calories: 331.6 | Total Fat: 5.7g | Saturated Fat: 0.5g | Cholesterol: 0mg | Sodium: 171.3mg | Potassium: 323mg | Total Carbohydrates: 69.4g | Dietary Fiber: 13.6g | Sugars: 32.2g | Protein: 6.7g

QUINOA SCRAMBLE

INGREDIENTS

8 eggs
1 Tbsp olive oil
1 cup cooked quinoa
3 cups fresh spinach
¼ cup feta cheese

DIRECTIONS

In a medium bowl, whisk the eggs together until well combined. In a medium nonstick pan, with olive oil over medium heat, cook the eggs until almost set but still very moist, stirring often with a rubber spatula.

Take eggs off the heat, stir in the quinoa, spinach and feta cheese and serve.

SERVES 4

PER SERVING
Calories: 281.8 | Total Fat: 19.5g | Saturated Fat: 5.9g | Cholesterol: 346.3mg | Sodium: 298.4mg | Potassium: 293.4mg | Total Carbohydrates: 10.4g | Dietary Fiber: 1.2g | Sugars: 2.2g | Protein: 15.7g

Lunch

MAKE MIDDAY MEALS A
BREEZE WITH THESE LIGHT,
NOURISHING FAVORITES.

Roasted
TOMATO AND FETA SOUP

INGREDIENTS

8 large tomatoes

4 cups vegetable stock (low-sodium or no-sodium)

1 tsp dried oregano

1 tsp dried cumin

6 oz crumbled feta cheese

DIRECTIONS

Preheat oven to 375 degrees F.

Place the tomatoes on a parchment-lined sheet pan and cook in the preheated oven for about 15 minutes, or until the tomatoes are softened and lightly browned.

In a large soup pot, add the cooked tomatoes, stock, oregano and cumin. Simmer for 15 to 20 minutes. Let the soup cool. Place soup in a blender and blend until smooth (you may have to blend in batches if your blender is not large enough).

Pour the soup back into the pot through a fine mesh sieve. Heat the soup and serve with an even amount of feta cheese on top.

SERVES 4

*Can be served with pita or flatbread

PER SERVING
Calories: 178.6 | Total Fat: 10.7g | Saturated Fat: 6.7g | Cholesterol: 39.6mg | Sodium: 483.5mg | Potassium: 651.1mg | Total Carbohydrates: 15.7g | Dietary Fiber: 2.9g | Sugars: 9.2g | Protein: 9.8g

Easy
GYROS

INGREDIENTS

4 whole-wheat pitas

8 oz prepared gyro meat (your favorite)

1 red onion, sliced

1 large tomato, sliced

½ cup tzatziki sauce

DIRECTIONS

Warm up the pita bread and gyro meat in a hot oven or in a hot pan.

Fill each pita with an even amount of meat, top with an even amount of onion and tomatoes, and drizzle with an even amount of sauce. Serve.

SERVES 4

PER SERVING
Calories: 315.4 | Total Fat: 13.5g | Saturated Fat: 6.4g |
Cholesterol: 17.5mg | Sodium: 650.2mg |
Potassium: 147.4mg | Total Carbohydrates: 40.4g |
Dietary Fiber: 5.1g | Sugars: 3.3g | Protein: 11.8g

LENTIL STEW

INGREDIENTS
1½ cups dry green lentils
1 (14.5-oz) can diced tomatoes, undrained
4 cups low-sodium vegetable stock
1 tsp dried oregano
2 Tbsp red wine vinegar

DIRECTIONS
Place the lentils, tomatoes, stock and oregano into a soup pot and bring to a boil. Lower the heat to a simmer and cook for about 40 minutes, or until the lentils are softened. Stir in the vinegar right before serving.

SERVES 4

*Can be served with Greek yogurt
on top as garnish*

PER SERVING
Calories: 119.8 | Total Fat: 0.3g | Saturated Fat: 0g |
Cholesterol: 0mg | Sodium: 266.5mg | Potassium: 375.2mg |
Total Carbohydrates: 22.2g | Dietary Fiber: 7g | Sugars: 6.4g |
Protein: 9.2g

ORANGE ANCHOVY SALAD

INGREDIENTS

2 oranges, segmented
1 can anchovies
1 lemon, juiced
1 head chicory lettuce
1 small red onion

DIRECTIONS

Segment the orange by cutting off each end. Set the oranges on a cutting board cut-side down. Using a sharp knife, starting at the top, cut all of the peel off, cutting down and continuing around the entire orange. Cut into the oranges between the pith (the white parts of the orange) to cut into segmented pieces.

Drain the anchovy oil into a bowl, add the lemon juice and whisk to combine.

Wash and dry the lettuce. Cut the lettuce leaves into bite-size pieces. Top with the segmented oranges, anchovies and red onions. Drizzle the desired amount of lemon dressing on the salad and serve.

SERVES 4

PER SERVING
Calories: 88.5 | Total Fat: 1.5g | Saturated Fat: 0.3g | Cholesterol: 9.6mg | Sodium: 442.2mg | Potassium: 649mg | Total Carbohydrates: 15.7g | Dietary Fiber: 7.1g | Sugars: 1.1g | Protein: 5.9g

TUNA
LETTUCE WRAPS

INGREDIENTS

1 head romaine or butter lettuce
1 (12-oz) can tuna, drained
1 (6.5-oz) jar artichoke hearts, chopped
6 oz canned white beans, mashed with fork
¾ cup Greek yogurt

DIRECTIONS

Wash and dry the lettuce. Take the lettuce leaves off the head and trim ends and remove any brown spots.

In a medium bowl, mix together the tuna, artichokes, white beans and yogurt.

Fill the desired amount of lettuce leaves with the tuna filling. Serve.

SERVES 4

PER SERVING
Calories: 143.1 | Total Fat: 5.3g | Saturated Fat: 1.1g | Cholesterol: 18.8mg | Sodium: 302.2mg | Potassium: 343.2mg | Total Carbohydrates: 14.4g | Dietary Fiber: 2g | Sugars: 1.7g | Protein: 11.6g

QUINOA
SHRIMP SALAD

INGREDIENTS
1 cup quinoa
¾ lb (23-27) shrimp, cooked
1 small bunch tender baby asparagus, chopped
½ red pepper, diced
½ cup Amba sauce (mango chutney)

DIRECTIONS
Bring 2 cups water to a boil in a medium pot. Rinse the quinoa in a fine mesh strainer. Place the rinsed quinoa in the boiling water, reduce to a simmer, place the lid on the pot and simmer for 15 to 20 minutes. Remove from heat and let sit for 10 minutes. Fluff with fork. Let cool.

Break off the woody ends of the asparagus and discard. Cut the remaining ends on a diagonal into small pieces.

In a large bowl, mix together the cooled quinoa, shrimp, asparagus, red pepper and chutney. Serve.

SERVE 4

PER SERVING
Calories: 348.3 | Total Fat: 3.9g | Saturated Fat: 0.4g | Cholesterol: 221mg | Sodium: 640.2mg | Potassium: 370.3mg | Total Carbohydrates: 47.4g | Dietary Fiber: 4.4g | Sugars: 16.7g | Protein: 31g

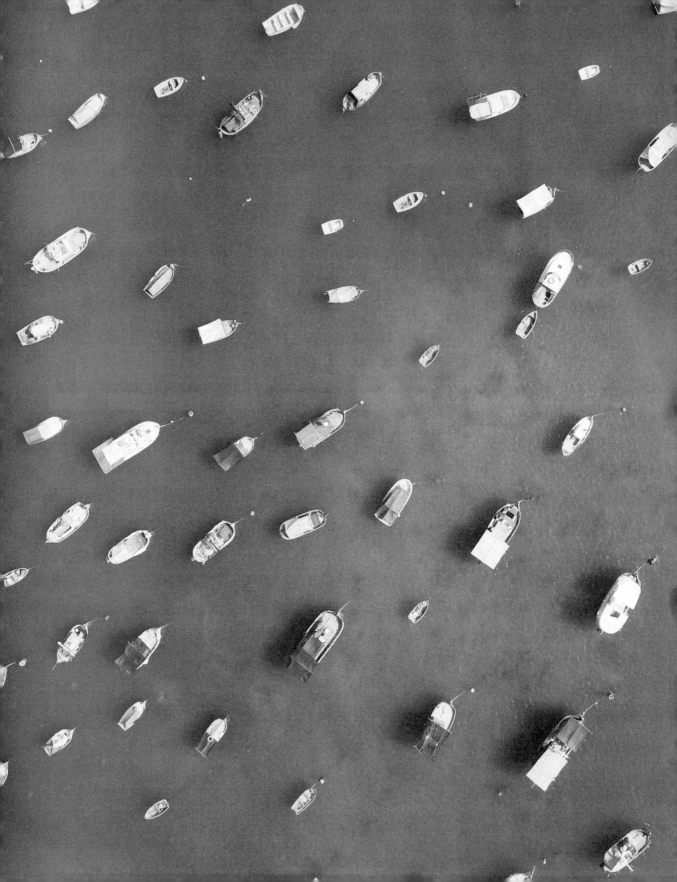

Open-Faced
SARDINE SANDWICH

INGREDIENTS

4 slices whole-wheat bread

1½ cups white beans

8 sardines, drained

1 small bunch beet greens

2 Tbsp chili-flavored olive oil

DIRECTIONS

Toast the bread. Add the beans to a medium bowl and smash with a fork until you achieve a chunky consistency. Place an even amount of beans onto each slice of toast. Top each with two sardines, an even amount of beet greens and a drizzle of chili olive oil. Serve.

SERVES 4

PER SERVING
Calories: 318.8 | Total Fat: 9.7g | Saturated Fat: 1g |
Cholesterol: 65.3mg | Sodium: 362.4mg |
Potassium: 795.2mg | Total Carbohydrates: 37.4g |
Dietary Fiber: 6.9g | Sugars: 1.5g | Protein: 21.2g

Mediterranean SALAD

INGREDIENTS

1 head romaine lettuce

½ English cucumber, sliced

   2 cups giardiniera
   (pickled vegetables), drained

6 oz crumbled feta cheese

½ cup green tahini sauce or
   green goddess dressing

DIRECTIONS

Wash and dry the lettuce. Place the lettuce on
a platter and arrange the cucumber, pickled
vegetables and feta on top. Drizzle with desired
amount of dressing and serve.

SERVES 4

PER SERVING
Calories: 315.8 | Total Fat: 25.6g | Saturated Fat: 7.4g |
Cholesterol: 37.8mg | Sodium: 1,527.8mg | Potassium: 82.6mg
| Total Carbohydrates: 7.3g | Dietary Fiber: 3.4g | Sugars 2.2g |
Protein: 9.6g

HUMMUS BOWL

INGREDIENTS

2 cups hummus

1 cup olive tapenade (your favorite)

¼ cup pumpkin seeds

2 Tbsp chili-flavored olive oil

4 whole-wheat pitas

DIRECTIONS

Place hummus evenly into four serving bowls. Top each bowl with an even amount of the tapenade and pumpkin seeds and drizzle each bowl with oil.

Serve with pita bread

SERVES 4

PER SERVING
Calories: 470.6 | Total Fat: 21.9g | Saturated Fat: 3.2g | Cholesterol: 0mg | Sodium: 997.2mg | Potassium: 430.6 mg | Total Carbohydrates: 56.2g | Dietary Fiber: 13.1g | Sugars: 1.8g | Protein: 16.9g

OCTOPUS SALAD

INGREDIENTS

2 lb octopus
1 lemon, juice and zest
⅓ cup, plus 1 Tbsp olive oil
2 Tbsp chopped capers
2 Tbsp minced fresh parsley

DIRECTIONS

Cut the octopus into 1½-inch pieces. In a large nonstick skillet, with 1 tablespoon olive oil over high heat, cook the octopus for about 30 seconds on each side, cooking in batches so as not to overcrowd the pan.

In a large bowl, mix together the lemon, lemon zest, oil, capers and parsley. Place the octopus into the dressing and toss to coat. Serve at room temperature.

SERVES 4

Can be served over lettuce

PER SERVING
Calories: 540.6 | Total Fat: 23.2g | Saturated Fat: 3.5g | Cholesterol: 217.6mg | Sodium: 1,079.5mg | Potassium: 1,477.7mg | Total Carbohydrates: 13g | Dietary Fiber: 1.3g | Sugars: 0g | Protein: 68g

Easy
FISH BAKE

INGREDIENTS
4 (4-oz) cod fillets
1 pint grape tomatoes
1 clove garlic, minced
½ cup low-sodium chicken stock
1 tsp red pepper flakes

DIRECTIONS
Preheat oven to 350 degrees F.

Place the fish in an oven-safe baking dish and add all ingredients on top of the fish. Place in the preheated oven and cook for 15 to 20 minutes, or until the fish is just cooked through. Serve.

SERVES 4

Can be served over rice

PER SERVING
Calories: 146 | Total Fat: 1.4g | Saturated Fat: 0.3g | Cholesterol: 63.3mg | Sodium: 131.4mg | Potassium: 329mg | Total Carbohydrates: 4.3g | Dietary Fiber: 0.7g | Sugars: 2.1g | Protein: 26.7g

CHICKPEA LETTUCE TACOS

INGREDIENTS
15 oz canned chickpeas
1 small red onion, sliced thin
2 tomatoes, diced
2 avocados, diced
1 head romaine lettuce

DIRECTIONS
Drain any liquid from the chickpeas.

In a medium bowl, mix together the onion, tomatoes and avocados.

Remove leaves from the head of lettuce (about 8 to 12). Wash and dry the leaves, and cut away the ends and brown spots.

Place desired amount of chickpeas into a piece of lettuce, top with desired amount of tomato mixture and serve.

SERVES 4

Season with salt and pepper if desired

PER SERVING
Calories: 156.6 | Total Fat: 7.8g | Saturated Fat: 0.9g | Cholesterol: 0mg | Sodium: 10.9mg | Potassium: 315mg | Total Carbohydrates: 18.9g | Dietary Fiber: 7.1g | Sugars: 1.9g | Protein: 5.1g

Grilled
LEMON CHICKEN CAESAR

INGREDIENTS
**2 boneless, skinless
  chicken breasts**
1 lemon, juice and zest
2 heads romaine lettuce
¼ cup Parmesan cheese
½ cup Caesar dressing

DIRECTIONS
Place the chicken in a container. Add the lemon juice and zest, and let the chicken marinate covered in the refrigerator for 1 hour.

Preheat grill.

Cut the lettuce in half, leaving the core intact, then thoroughly wash and dry the lettuce.

Place the chicken on the preheated grill and cook for 3 to 4 minutes on each side, or until the chicken is cooked through (internal temperature of 165 degrees F). Remove the chicken from the grill and let rest for 7 minutes. Slice the chicken.

Place the lettuce, cut-side down, into the hot grill and grill until grill marks have been achieved and the lettuce is partially wilted. Place the lettuce on plates. Top with chicken, cheese and the desired amount of dressing. Serve.

SERVES 4

PER SERVING
Calories: 211.8 | Total Fat: 5.1g | Saturated Fat: 1g | Cholesterol: 78.1mg | Sodium: 207.8mg | Potassium: 56.9mg | Total Carbohydrates: 8.6g | Dietary Fiber: 1.1g | Sugars: 0.5g | Protein: 30.7g

Shrimp Stuffed
PITA HOT POCKET

INGREDIENTS

4 whole-wheat pitas
¾ lb (23–70) cooked shrimp, tails removed
8 oz fresh spinach
1 cup chopped roasted red peppers
8 oz mozzarella cheese

DIRECTIONS

Stuff each pita evenly with all ingredients.
Place the stuffed pitas in a large nonstick pan on
medium heat with a cover. Cook until the cheese
has melted, flipping once during cooking. Serve.

SERVES 4

PER SERVING
Calories: 282.1 | Total Fat: 13.6g | Saturated Fat: 6.7g |
Cholesterol: 140.5mg | Sodium: 561.4mg | Potassium: 214mg |
Total Carbohydrates: 13.3g | Dietary Fiber: 4.5g | Sugars: 0.5g
| Protein: 25.3g

Garden
VEGETABLE GAZPACHO

INGREDIENTS

1 large bowl assorted chopped
   vegetables (your favorites)
1 clove garlic
1 Tbsp freshly ground black pepper
3 slices whole-wheat bread
4 cups low-sodium vegetable broth

DIRECTIONS

Place all ingredients into a blender and blend
until smooth. Pour through a fine mesh sieve and
chill. Serve.

SERVES 4

PER SERVING
Calories: 133.3 | Total Fat: 6.9g | Saturated Fat: 0.9g |
Cholesterol: 0mg | Sodium: 197.6mg | Potassium: 3mg |
Total Carbohydrates: 15.2g | Dietary Fiber: 4.3g | Sugars: 5.5g |
Protein: 13g

PITA BREAD PIZZA

INGREDIENTS

4 whole-grain pitas or flatbreads
½ cup tzatziki sauce
8 oz cooked salmon, broken into small pieces
1 small red onion, thinly sliced
2 tsp capers

DIRECTIONS

Toast the bread on a hot grill or in a hot pan until lightly browned and crispy. Spread an even amount of tzatziki sauce onto each. Top evenly with remaining ingredients and serve.

SERVES 4

PER SERVING
Calories: 298.1 | Total Fat: 7.3g | Saturated Fat: 0.8g |
Cholesterol: 31.3mg | Sodium: 400.7mg |
Potassium: 413.6mg | Total Carbohydrates: 36.7g |
Dietary Fiber: 5.1g | Sugars: 2.6g | Protein: 20.7g

Sides

ALL YOU NEED TO ROUND OUT
ANY MEAL IS THE PERFECT
COMPLEMENTARY DISH, LIKE
ONE OF THESE!

Greek
SWEET POTATO FRIES

INGREDIENTS

4 sweet potatoes

2 Tbsp olive oil

**6 fresh mint leaves,
   julienned**

**3 oz crumbled
   feta cheese**

½ cup tzatziki sauce

DIRECTIONS

Preheat oven to
375 degrees F.

Wash the sweet
potatoes thoroughly.
Cut the potatoes into
steak fry–style french
fries. Place the french
fries on a parchment-
lined baking sheet.
Drizzle with oil, mix
to coat all french fries
with oil and arrange
the potatoes evenly
around the baking
sheet in a single layer.
Place on the middle
rack of preheated
oven and cook for
15 to 20 minutes, or
until the potatoes are
soft in the middle and
lightly browned on
the outside.

Place the potatoes
in a serving dish and
sprinkle with mint
and feta. Serve with
tzatziki sauce on the
side for dipping.

SERVES 4

*Season fries with
salt when taken out
of oven*

PER SERVING
Calories: 259.5 | Total Fat:
8.9g | Saturated Fat: 4.6g |
Cholesterol: 25.2mg |
Sodium: 334.3mg |
Potassium: 282.8mg |
Total Carbohydrates: 37g |
Dietary Fiber: 4.3g |
Sugars: 6.6g | Protein: 8.2g

Roasted
RED ONIONS

INGREDIENTS
4 red onions, cut into 1" rounds,
   skins attached
2 pears, diced
3 oz crumbled feta cheese
¼ cup pine nuts
¼ cup balsamic vinegar

DIRECTIONS
Preheat oven to 375 degrees F.

Place the onion rounds on a parchment-lined baking sheet and cook in the preheated oven for about 15 minutes, or until the onions are softened. Place onions on a serving dish, top the onions evenly with pears, feta, pine nuts and a drizzle of balsamic vinegar. Serve.

SERVES 4

PER SERVING
Calories: 237.3 | Total Fat: 12.2g | Saturated Fat: 4.7g |
Cholesterol: 25.2mg | Sodium: 326.1mg |
Potassium: 407.6mg | Total Carbohydrates: 27.8g |
Dietary Fiber: 5.2g | Sugars: 15.9g | Protein: 7.2g

Wild RICE SALAD

INGREDIENTS
1½ cups wild rice
⅓ cup finely chopped beets
4 kale leaves, finely chopped
2 carrots, finely chopped
¼ cup Greek vinaigrette

DIRECTIONS
Cook the wild rice according to package directions. Let cool.

In a medium bowl, mix together the cooled rice and remaining ingredients. Serve.

SERVES 4

PER SERVING
Calories: 112.1 | Total Fat: 2.8g | Saturated Fat: 0.5g |
Cholesterol: 0mg | Sodium: 271.6mg |
Potassium: 150.3mg | Total Carbohydrates: 19.1g |
Dietary Fiber: 2.5g | Sugars: 4.3g | Protein: 3.5g

Charred
CABBAGE, BEET AND ORANGE SALAD

INGREDIENTS
4 large slices red cabbage
1 red onion, sliced
2 medium roasted beets, sliced
1 large orange, peeled and sliced
¼ cup prepared Greek vinaigrette

DIRECTIONS
Preheat grill to medium-high heat.

Place the cabbage on a well-greased, preheated grill and cook for about 3 minutes on each side, or until lightly charred and wilted.

Place cabbage onto a serving plate and top with onions, beets and oranges. Drizzle with the desired amount of vinaigrette. Serve.

SERVES 4

PER SERVING
Calories: 146.9 | Total Fat: 8.9g | Saturated Fat: 0g |
Cholesterol: 0mg | Sodium: 213.5mg |
Potassium: 438.9mg | Total Carbohydrates: 15.1g |
Dietary Fiber: 4.3g | Sugars: 9.4g | Protein: 2.4g

ZA'ATAR BULGUR
with Zucchini

INGREDIENTS
1½ cups bulgur
2 Tbsp olive oil
1 tsp za'atar
1 onion, diced
2 small zucchini, sliced

DIRECTIONS
Cook the bulgur according to package directions with the water seasoned with za'atar.

In a large skillet with oil, cook the zucchini until tender, add the garlic and continue to cook for another minute.

In a large bowl, mix together the bulgur and zucchini and serve.

SERVES 4

PER SERVING
Calories: 239.5 | Total Fat: 7.3g | Saturated Fat: 1g | Cholesterol: 0mg | Sodium: 13.7mg | Potassium: 492.8mg | Total Carbohydrates: 40.6g | Dietary Fiber: 10.4g | Sugars: 3.2g | Protein: 6.7g

Creamy
LENTILS

INGREDIENTS

1 cup green lentils, picked through and rinsed

1 onion, diced

2 cups baby spinach

6 fresh mint leaves, chopped

¼ cup Greek yogurt

DIRECTIONS

In a medium soup pot, bring 2 cups water, lentils, spinach and mint to a boil. Lower the heat and simmer for about 30 minutes, or until the lentils are softened. Swirl in the yogurt and serve.

SERVES 4

PER SERVING
Calories: 82.5 | Total Fat: 1.1g | Saturated Fat: 0.6g | Cholesterol: 3.1mg | Sodium: 22.7mg | Potassium: 322.6mg | Total Carbohydrates: 13g | Dietary Fiber: 4.6g | Sugars: 2.6g | Protein: 5.7g

GRILLED ZUCCHINI
with Tomato Salad

INGREDIENTS
4 baby zucchini
3 Tbsp olive oil
3 tomatoes, seeded and chopped
1 red onion, thinly sliced
2 Tbsp red wine vinegar

DIRECTIONS
Preheat grill to medium-high heat.

Wash and dry the zucchini, cut the zucchini in half lengthwise. Brush with olive oil and place on the preheated grill, cut-side down. Cook for 5 to 7 minutes, or until grill marks are achieved and the zucchini is tender.

In a medium bowl, add remaining oil and vinegar and mix to combine. Add the tomatoes and onions and toss to coat.

Take the zucchini off the grill and top with tomato salad. Serve.

SERVES 4

PER SERVING
Calories: 117.8 | Total Fat: 10.5g | Saturated Fat: 1.4g | Cholesterol: 0mg | Sodium: 9.2mg | Potassium: 292.8mg | Total Carbohydrates: 6.1g | Dietary Fiber: 1.5g | Sugars: 0.7g | Protein: 1.3g

ROASTED VEGETABLES
with Feta

INGREDIENTS
2 cups each assorted vegetables (red peppers, zucchini, asparagus, red onion, etc.)

2 Tbsp olive oil

1 tsp oregano

1 cup low-sodium marinara sauce

3 oz crumbled feta cheese

DIRECTIONS
Preheat oven to 375 degrees F.

Cut all vegetables in larger-than-bite-size pieces. Place the vegetables on a parchment-lined baking sheet. Drizzle with oil and season with oregano, then toss to mix. Place in the preheated oven and cook for 15 to 20 minutes, or until the vegetables are softened.

In a large bowl, mix the cooked vegetables and marinara sauce, top with feta and serve.

SERVES 4

PER SERVING
Calories: 185.7 | Total Fat: 13.6g | Saturated Fat: 5.2g | Cholesterol: 25.2mg | Sodium: 333.9mg | Potassium: 23.8mg | Total Carbohydrates: 10.4g | Dietary Fiber: 2.2g | Sugars: 6.2g | Protein: 5.6g

Simple MEDITERRANEAN SALAD

INGREDIENTS

2 cups prepared white beans

1 pint grape tomatoes, sliced in half

¼ cup chopped fresh parsley

3 oz crumbled feta cheese

¼ cup Greek vinaigrette

DIRECTIONS

Add all ingredients in a large bowl and toss. Serve.

SERVES 4

PER SERVING
Calories: 269.1 | Total Fat: 8.9g | Saturated Fat: 4.8g |
Cholesterol: 25.2mg | Sodium: 504.5mg |
Potassium: 628.1mg | Total Carbohydrates: 34.1g |
Dietary Fiber: 6.9g | Sugars: 4.1g | Protein: 14.1g

Herb
FAVA BEAN SALAD

INGREDIENTS
4 cups fava beans
½ cup pesto
¼ cup chopped fresh parsley
¼ cup chopped fresh mint
2 oz arugula lettuce

DIRECTIONS
Boil the beans in salted water for 5 to 10 minutes, or until the beans are tender. Drain.

Using a sharp knife, make a small slit in the skin of each bean. Peel and discard the skin.

In a medium bowl, add beans and the remaining ingredients and toss to coat. Serve.

SERVES 4

PER SERVING
Calories: 285.6 | Total Fat: 16.2g | Saturated Fat: 2.7g |
Cholesterol: 7.5mg | Sodium: 356.6mg | Potassium: 534mg |
Total Carbohydrates: 28g | Dietary Fiber: 2.6g |
Sugars: 12.2g | Protein: 13.9g

Red
RICE

INGREDIENTS

2 cups rice
1 onion, diced
2 cloves garlic, chopped
1 (6-oz) can tomato paste
1 Tbsp oregano

DIRECTIONS

In a medium heavy-bottomed saucepan, bring 4 cups water to a boil. Add all ingredients to the pot and lower the heat. Simmer with a lid on for 20 minutes.

Fluff the rice with a fork and serve.

SERVES 4

PER SERVING
Calories: 132.3 | Total Fat: 0.5g | Saturated Fat: 0.1g | Cholesterol: 0mg | Sodium: 169.8mg | Potassium: 295.2mg | Total Carbohydrates: 29g | Dietary Fiber: 2.1g | Sugars: 3.4g | Protein: 3.5g

Lemon
SWEET POTATO SALAD

INGREDIENTS
2 lb sweet potatoes, cut into 1" pieces
2 lemons, juice and zest
½ tsp dried dill
¼ cup chopped fresh parsley
½ cup Greek yogurt

DIRECTIONS
Bring a large pot of salted water with potatoes to a boil. Cook until the potatoes are fork-tender, about 8 minutes.

In a large bowl, mix together the lemon juice and zest, dill, parsley and yogurt. Add the cooked potatoes to the bowl and mix to combine (add more yogurt if necessary). Serve.

SERVES 4

PER SERVING
Calories: 214.2 | Total Fat: 2.2g | Saturated Fat: 1.2g |
Polyunsaturated Fat: 0.2g | Monounsaturated Fat: 0.0g |
Cholesterol: 6.3mg | Sodium: 93.1mg | Potassium: 1,065.4mg |
Total Carbohydrates: 46.4g | Dietary Fiber: 8g |
Sugars: 14.9g | Protein: 5.6g

Herb Ricotta
STUFFED TOMATOES

INGREDIENTS

4 tomatoes

2 cups ricotta cheese

1 Tbsp Italian seasoning mix

1 clove garlic, minced

¼ cup Parmesan cheese

DIRECTIONS

Preheat oven to 375 degrees F.

Cut the tops off each tomato. Hollow out the tomatoes and set onto a parchment-lined baking pan.

Place ricotta cheese in a blender and blend until light, fluffy and smooth. In a medium bowl, fold together ricotta cheese, seasoning and garlic.

Stuff each tomato evenly with the mixture and top each stuffed tomato with Parmesan cheese.

Place tomatoes in the preheated oven and cook for 15 minutes, or until the tomato is softened and the cheese is heated through.

SERVES 4

Additional ingredients can be added to stuffing if desired

PER SERVING
Calories: 276.6 | Total Fat: 17.8g | Saturated Fat: 11.4g | Cholesterol: 67.7mg | Sodium: 219.8mg | Potassium: 569.8mg | Total Carbohydrates: 11.2g | Dietary Fiber: 2g | Sugars: 5.3g | Protein: 18.5g

Dinner

YOU'LL BE SMILING AS THE SUN
SETS KNOWING YOU'VE GOT
THESE DISHES ON DECK.

Easy
CHICKEN MARSALA POCKETS

INGREDIENTS

8 large chicken thighs
½ cup Marsala wine
**8 oz sliced baby bella
    mushrooms**
**2 cloves garlic,
    chopped**
**½ tsp chopped dried
    thyme**

DIRECTIONS

Preheat oven or grill to 375 degrees F or medium-high heat.

Making four pockets with four pieces of foil, place two chicken thighs onto each piece of foil large enough to wrap the chicken. Place an even amount of wine, mushrooms, garlic and thyme into each pocket. Wrap the pocket tightly closed, turning the edges of foil together in a tight fold.

Place on the hot grill or oven and cook for 20 to 30 minutes, or until the chicken is cooked through (internal temperature of 165 degrees F). Serve.

SERVES 4

*Season with salt
and pepper if desired
*Can be served
over rice, noodles
or potatoes

PER SERVING
Calories: 257.4 | Total Fat: 15g | Saturated Fat: 4.5g | Cholesterol: 80mg | Sodium: 353.1mg | Potassium: 21.8mg | Total Carbohydrates: 4.6g | Dietary Fiber: 0.9g | Sugars: 0.8g | Protein: 19.4g

HALIBUT SKEWERS
with Tahini Sauce

INGREDIENTS
1 lb halibut, cut into 1" pieces
4 small zucchini, sliced
1 pint grape tomatoes
1 large red onion, cut into 1" pieces
⅓ cup prepared tahini

DIRECTIONS
Preheat grill to medium-high heat.

Skewer the fish, zucchini, tomatoes and red onion
in a uniform fashion on metal skewers or on
wooden skewers that have been soaked in water.

Place skewers onto a well-greased, hot grill and
cook for a few minutes on each side, or until the
fish is just cooked through. Place the skewers
onto a serving platter, drizzle with tahini sauce
and serve.

SERVES 4

PER SERVING
Calories: 314.8 | Total Fat: 13.5g | Saturated Fat: 1.9g |
Cholesterol: 46.5mg | Sodium: 103.7mg |
Potassium: 1,020.9mg | Total Carbohydrates: 14g |
Dietary Fiber: 4.2g | Sugars: 5.3g | Protein: 35g

FRIED WHOLE SEA BASS
with Lemon Pan Sauce

INGREDIENTS
**4 whole sea bass (1½–
    2 lb each), cleaned
    and gutted***
3 Tbsp olive oil
2 lemons, juiced
2 tsp capers
2 cloves garlic, minced

DIRECTIONS
Pat the fish dry with paper towels. With a sharp knife, cut the fish on a diagonal to the bone every 2 inches on both sides.

In a large pan with oil over medium-high heat, fry the fish until the skin is crisp. Turn the fish and cook on the other side until the fish is just cooked through (no longer opaque in the middle).

Remove the fish from the pan and drain the oil. Turn the heat to medium-low and add the lemon juice and capers to pan. Let cook a couple of minutes to reduce. Pour the sauce into a serving dish and top with the cooked fish. Serve immediately.

SERVES 4

**Season fish with
salt and pepper
before frying*

PER SERVING
Calories: 198.7 | Total Fat: 9.5g | Saturated Fat: 1.6g | Cholesterol: 53.5mg | Sodium: 142.2mg | Potassium: 415.6mg | Total Carbohydrates: 6.3g | Dietary Fiber: 2.6g | Sugars: 0g | Protein: 24.6g

Comfort
BEEF AND RICE DINNER

INGREDIENTS
¾ cup rice
1 lb ground beef
  (you can substitute ground veal)
1 cup marinara sauce (your favorite)
1 cup halved green olives
1 cup beef broth

DIRECTIONS
In a medium pot, bring 1½ cups water to a boil.
Stir in the rice and cover, lower the heat to a simmer
and cook for 20 minutes. Uncover the rice and fluff
with a fork.

Meanwhile, in a large nonstick pan, cook the ground
beef until browned and cooked through. Add in the
marinara sauce, olives, broth and cooked rice. Turn
up the heat to medium and cook for another 3 to 5
minutes (add more broth or sauce if needed). Serve.

SERVES 4

Season with salt and pepper if desired

PER SERVING
Calories: 593.3 | Total Fat: 26.4g | Saturated Fat: 9.7g |
Cholesterol: 85.1mg | Sodium: 610.7mg | Potassium: 528.3mg |
Total Carbohydrates: 59.3g | Dietary Fiber: 1g |
Sugars: 3.1g | Protein: 26.1g

SALMON
with Olive Tapenade

INGREDIENTS
4 (4–6-oz) salmon fillets
1 Tbsp olive oil
1 large tomato, thinly sliced
½ cup olive tapenade
2 cups prepared wild rice

DIRECTIONS
Preheat oven to 375 degrees F.

Place the salmon fillets in an oven-safe baking
dish with olive oil. Top each salmon fillet with
two slices of tomatoes and an even amount of
tapenade.

Place in the preheated oven and cook for
about 15 minutes, or until the fish is just
cooked through.

Place the salmon on top of the prepared rice
and serve.

SERVES 4

PER SERVING
Calories: 295.5 | Total Fat: 12g | Saturated Fat: 1.6g |
Cholesterol: 62.7mg | Sodium: 55.9mg | Potassium: 738.5mg |
Total Carbohydrates: 19.6g | Dietary Fiber: 2.5g |
Sugars: 0.6g | Protein: 26.2g

Roasted EGGPLANT BAKE

INGREDIENTS

6 medium eggplants
3 Tbsp olive oil
1 lb sliced mushrooms
3 cups marinara sauce
  (your favorite)
1 Tbsp cinnamon

DIRECTIONS

Preheat oven to 350 degrees F.

Slice the eggplants into thin rounds. Brush the eggplant slices with olive oil and place on parchment-lined baking sheets. Place the eggplant in the preheated oven and cook for 10 to 15 minutes, or until the eggplant has softened and is lightly browned.

In a dry large nonstick skillet over medium heat, cook the mushrooms, stirring often, until softened. Set aside.

In a medium bowl, mix together the cinnamon with the marinara sauce.

In a medium to large baking dish, add sauce to the bottom of the baking dish, layer with eggplant to cover the sauce, add a layer of sauce on top of the eggplant layer and top with a layer of cooked mushrooms. Repeat layering until all ingredients are used, leaving sauce for the final layer.

Place on the middle rack of the oven and cook for 30 to 40 minutes, or until the sauce is bubbling and the eggplant is heated through. Take out of the oven and let set for 5 minutes. Cut and serve.

SERVES 4

Mozzarella, feta or Parmesan cheese can be added to the bake if desired

PER SERVING
Calories: 293.9 | Total Fat: 12.8g |
Saturated Fat: 1.8g | Cholesterol:
0mg | Sodium: 275.9mg |
Potassium: 1,659.7mg |
Total Carbohydrates: 43.9g |
Dietary Fiber: 17.3g |
Sugars: 24.3g | Protein: 8.2g

Creamy
CHICKEN DINNER SKILLET

INGREDIENTS

4 boneless, skinless chicken breasts
1 Tbsp olive oil
1 cup chopped roasted red peppers
2 cups fresh spinach
3 cups sliced mushrooms, divided

DIRECTIONS

Season chicken with salt and pepper. Then, in a large nonstick skillet with oil over medium heat, cook the chicken about 4 minutes on each side, or until the chicken is just slightly undercooked. Remove the chicken from the pan and set aside.

Take 1 cup of mushrooms with ½ cup water in a blender and blend until smooth. Place in the skillet, add the red peppers, spinach and remaining mushrooms, then bring the mixture to a simmer. Place the chicken back into the skillet and cook another couple of minutes, or until the chicken is cooked through (internal temperature of 165 degrees F). Serve.

SERVES 4

Season chicken with salt and pepper before cooking
Can be served with a desired amount of Parmesan cheese
Can be served over pasta, rice or noodles

PER SERVING
Calories: 192.2 | Total Fat: 6.7g | Saturated Fat: 1.3g | Cholesterol: 70.2mg | Sodium: 75.4mg | Potassium: 526.8mg | Total Carbohydrates: 4.6g | Dietary Fiber: 1.7g | Sugars: 2.7g | Protein: 28.1g

PASTA WITH TOMATOES AND PEAS

INGREDIENTS

2 cups low-carb campanelle pasta

2 cloves garlic, minced

2 large ripe tomatoes, diced

2 Tbsp olive oil

1 cup peas (fresh or frozen)

DIRECTIONS

In a large pot of salted boiling water, cook the pasta according to package directions for al dente. Drain the pasta, reserving ½ cup pasta water.

In a large skillet, add the remaining ingredients and cook on medium heat until the tomatoes are softened. Add in the drained pasta and stir to combine. Add in the pasta water, let cook another minute and serve.

SERVES 4

Bacon can be added to the recipe
Alternative pasta works well in this recipe
Can be served with grated Parmesan cheese if desired

PER SERVING
Calories: 212.6 | Total Fat: 7.7g | Saturated Fat: 1g | Cholesterol: 0mg | Sodium: 48.6mg | Potassium: 258.7mg | Total Carbohydrates: 29.9g | Dietary Fiber: 3.5g | Sugars: 2.8g | Protein: 6.2g

YOGURT
COD BAKE

INGREDIENTS
½ cup Greek yogurt
1 tsp dried dill
1 lemon, juiced
4 (4–6-oz) cod fillets
1 Tbsp olive oil

DIRECTIONS
Preheat oven to 375 degrees F.

In a medium bowl, mix together the yogurt, dill and lemon juice.

Coat the bottom of an oven-safe baking dish with oil. Place the cod fillets into the baking dish. Spoon an even amount of yogurt mixture on top of each cod fillet.

Place in the preheated oven and cook for 15 to 20 minutes, or until the fish is just cooked through. Serve.

SERVES 4

PER SERVING
Calories: 182 | Total Fat: 6.2g | Saturated Fat: 1.7g |
Cholesterol: 68.7mg | Sodium: 108.5mg | Potassium:
381.5mg | Total Carbohydrates: 4.9g | Dietary Fiber: 1.3g |
Sugars: 1.9g | Protein: 26.8g

Tabbouleh-Stuffed
TOMATO SALAD

INGREDIENTS
5.25 oz store-bought tabbouleh
5 large ripe tomatoes
1 lemon, juiced
2 Tbsp olive oil
4 large bib lettuce leaves

DIRECTIONS
Cook the tabbouleh according to package directions.

Hollow out the tomatoes by cutting the top off and spooning out any flesh and seeds. Chop the flesh of the tomatoes.

In a large bowl, mix together the cooked tabbouleh, chopped tomatoes, lemon juice and olive oil.

Stuff each tomato with the tabbouleh mixture and place the stuffed tomatoes onto a bib lettuce leaf and serve.

SERVES 4

*Cooked chicken or fish can be added if desired

PER SERVING
Calories: 140.6 | Total Fat: 6.6g | Saturated Fat: 0.5g | Cholesterol: 0mg | Sodium: 5.6mg | Potassium: 172.9mg | Total Carbohydrates: 21.3g | Dietary Fiber: 6.5g | Sugars: 1.3g | Protein: 4.3g

SEARED SCALLOPS
with Avocado Mint Sauce

INGREDIENTS
2 lb sea scallops
½ cup prepared
  guacamole
½ cup Greek yogurt
¼ cup chopped
  fresh mint
2 Tbsp olive oil

DIRECTIONS
Clean, rinse and pat the scallops dry with paper towels. Set aside.

Place the guacamole, yogurt and mint into a blender and blend until smooth.

Season scallops with salt and pepper before cooking. In a nonstick pan or cast-iron pan with oil, fry the scallops on high heat until scallops are seared (golden brown) on each side and are no longer opaque.

Place the avocado sauce onto a platter and place the seared scallops on top. Serve.

SERVES 4

Season sauce with salt and pepper if desired

PER SERVING
Calories: 195.4 | Total Fat: 12.8g | Saturated Fat: 2.1g | Cholesterol: 31mg | Sodium: 190.8mg | Potassium: 299.2mg | Total Carbohydrates: 5.9g | Dietary Fiber: 1.3g | Sugars: 1.9g | Protein: 14.2g

EGGPLANT STEW

INGREDIENTS

3 Tbsp olive oil
4 medium eggplants, peeled, cut into 1" pieces
28 oz canned tomatoes
4 cups low-sodium vegetable stock
½ tsp paprika

DIRECTIONS

In a large dutch oven or heavy-bottomed soup pot with olive oil over medium-high heat, cook the eggplant until lightly browned and softened, stirring often, about 10 minutes. Add in the tomatoes, stock and paprika. Lower the heat and simmer for 10 to 15 minutes. Serve.

SERVES 4

Any style beans or potatoes can be added if desired
Season with salt and pepper if desired

PER SERVING
Calories: 252.3 | Total Fat: 8.3g | Saturated Fat: 1.2g | Cholesterol: 0mg | Sodium: 268.9mg | Potassium: 1,594.5mg | Total Carbohydrates: 43.9g | Dietary Fiber: 15.4g | Sugars: 22.4g | Protein: 8.8g

FETTUCCINE WITH GARLIC
and Toasted Bread Crumbs

INGREDIENTS
¾ box low-carb
    fettuccine
3 Tbsp olive oil
4 cloves garlic,
    chopped
1 Tbsp red
    pepper flakes
3 cup whole-wheat
    seasoned
    bread crumbs

DIRECTIONS
In a large pot of salted boiling water, cook the pasta according to package directions for al dente. Drain the pasta, reserving ½ cup pasta water.

In a dry nonstick pan over medium-low heat, lightly toast the bread crumbs, stirring often. Remove from heat and set aside.

In a large skillet with oil over medium-low heat, cook the garlic and red pepper for 1 minute. Add pasta and pasta water and let cook another couple of minutes, mixing to combine.

Place the pasta into a large bowl, add the toasted breadcrumbs and toss to combine. Serve.

SERVES 4

*Alternative pasta works well in this recipe
*Parmesan cheese can be added if desired

PER SERVING
Calories: 224.3 | Total Fat: 4.7g | Saturated Fat: 0.5g | Cholesterol: 0mg | Sodium: 40.5mg | Potassium: 60mg | Total Carbohydrates: 25g | Dietary Fiber: 9.1g | Sugars: 3g | Protein: 29g

Easy
GRILLED PORK CHOPS

INGREDIENTS
1 tsp salt
1 tsp pepper
1 Tbsp oregano
2 lemons, juiced
**4 6-oz bone-in pork chops (can be substituted
  with veal)**

DIRECTIONS
In a medium bowl, mix together salt, pepper,
oregano, lemon juice and ⅓ cup water. Pour the
marinade over the pork and marinate for at least
1 hour in the refrigerator.

Preheat grill to medium-high. Take the pork out
of the refrigerator and place on the hot grill.
Cook for 3 to 4 minutes on each side, or until
the internal temperature reaches 145 degrees F.
Take the pork off the grill and let rest for 5 to 7
minutes. Serve.

SERVES 4

PER SERVING
Calories: 347.2 | Total Fat: 15.5g | Saturated Fat: 5.7g |
Cholesterol: 134.3mg | Sodium: 151.9mg | Potassium:
673.6mg | Total Carbohydrates: 3.6g | Dietary Fiber: 1.8g |
Sugars: 0g | Protein: 47.3g

Seafood
RICE SKILLET

INGREDIENTS
2 cups rice
1 onion, diced
2 tomatoes, diced
⅛ tsp saffron threads
2 lb assorted shellfish (shrimp, scallops, whitefish)

DIRECTIONS
Preheat oven to 350 degrees F.

In a large oven-safe skillet with a lid, add 4 cups water or chicken broth, rice, onion, tomatoes and saffron. Mix to combine. Bring rice to a full boil on high heat, then place the skillet in the preheated oven, covered tightly with the lid, and cook for 20 minutes.

Place the seafood into the skillet with rice, pushing the seafood into the rice, and continue to cook with the lid on until all seafood is cooked through, about 10 minutes. Serve.

SERVES 4

PER SERVING
Calories: 148.5 | Total Fat: 0.5g | Saturated Fat: 0.1g |
Cholesterol: 21.5mg | Sodium: 29.3mg | Potassium: 157.9mg |
Total Carbohydrates: 30.3g | Dietary Fiber: 1.1g |
Sugars: 0.7g | Protein: 5.1g

EGGPLANT ROLLUPS

INGREDIENTS

2 medium eggplants

3 cups marinara sauce (your favorite)

3 oz fresh spinach

2 cups sliced roasted red peppers

2 cups chopped jarred artichoke hearts

DIRECTIONS

Slice eggplants into thin strips cut lengthwise. Sprinkle each slice of eggplant with salt and set in a colander to drain for 30 minutes. Rinse the salt off.

Preheat oven to 350 degrees F.

Place half of the marinara sauce into the bottom of an oven-safe baking dish.

Place an even amount of spinach, peppers and artichokes onto the sliced eggplant and roll the eggplants. Place the stuffed eggplant rolls edge-side up in the baking dish. Place the remaining sauce on top of the eggplant rolls and cook in the preheated oven for about 30 minutes, or until the sauce is bubbling and the rolls are heated through. Serve.

SERVES 4

Mozzarella and Parmesan cheese can be added to the recipe if desired

PER SERVING
Calories: 226 | Total Fat: 7.5g | Saturated Fat: 0.5g | Cholesterol: 0mg | Sodium: 794mg | Potassium: 1,440.9mg | Total Carbohydrates: 38.5g | Dietary Fiber: 11.3g | Sugars: 18g | Protein: 7g

WHITE BEAN
AND TUNA BOWL

INGREDIENTS

2 cups cooked white beans
2 cans tuna, drained
2 large tomatoes, chopped
4 hard-boiled eggs, sliced
½ cup tzatziki sauce (your favorite)

DIRECTIONS

In four serving bowls, add an equal amount
of cooked beans. Top each bowl with tuna,
tomatoes and hard-boiled eggs in a decorative
manner. Drizzle each with a generous amount of
tzatziki sauce. Serve.

SERVES 4

PER SERVING
Calories: 340.8 | Total Fat: 7.8g | Saturated Fat: 2.2g |
Cholesterol: 217.1mg | Sodium: 372.2mg | Potassium:
347.9mg | Total Carbohydrates: 34.1g | Dietary Fiber: 1.5g |
Sugars: 2.2g | Protein: 34.8g

SALMON
with Balsamic Onions

INGREDIENTS
2 Tbsp olive oil
2 large onions, sliced
½ tsp fresh thyme
½ cup balsamic
4 6-oz salmon fillets*

DIRECTIONS
Place the onions and thyme in a large nonstick frying pan with 1 tablespoon oil over medium-low heat. Cook the onions for 10 to 15 minutes, stirring frequently, until the onions are soft. Add the vinegar and continue to cook until the vinegar has reduced by half and has thickened. Lower the heat to warm.

In a large nonstick skillet with remaining oil over medium-high heat, cook the salmon fillets for about 4 minutes on each side, or until the fish is just cooked through.

Plate the salmon and top with balsamic onions. Serve.

SERVES 4

Season salmon fillets with salt and pepper before cooking

PER SERVING
Calories: 856.4 | Total Fat: 81.6g | Saturated Fat: 11.1g | Cholesterol: 62.7mg | Sodium: 57.9mg | Potassium: 673.6mg | Total Carbohydrates: 9g | Dietary Fiber: 1.4g | Sugars: 3.2g | Protein: 23.4g

PORK MEATBALL
AND PINEAPPLE SKEWERS

INGREDIENTS
¾ lb ground pork
2 slices bread, crust removed, chopped
¼ cup Greek yogurt
2 Tbsp finely chopped fresh mint
1 cup pineapple, cut into ½" pieces

DIRECTIONS
In a large bowl, mix together the pork, bread, yogurt and mint until just mixed through. Make 1½-inch meatballs.

Preheat grill to medium-high heat.

Place the meatballs and pineapples onto a metal skewer, alternating meatball then pineapple.

Place the skewers onto the well-greased, preheated grill. Cook for about 10 minutes, or until the meat is cooked through, turning during cooking. Serve.

SERVES 4

Can be served over salad or rice

PER SERVING
Calories: 290.7 | Total Fat: 19.5g | Saturated Fat: 7.4g |
Cholesterol: 64.4mg | Sodium: 118.7mg | Potassium: 329.4mg |
Total Carbohydrates: 11.9g | Dietary Fiber: 0.8g |
Sugars: 5.5g | Protein: 16.2g

EGGPLANT MEATBALLS

INSTRUCTIONS
3 medium eggplants, peeled, diced
2 eggs
2 oz feta cheese
1 onion, diced
1 tsp oregano

Preheat oven to 375 degrees F.

Place the diced eggplant, eggs, feta, onion
and oregano in a food processor and pulse
until mixture becomes a chunky, meat-like
consistency. Make golf ball–size balls from the
mixture and place on a parchment-lined baking
sheet. Place in the preheated oven and cook
for 15 to 20 minutes, or until the meatballs are
browned on the outside and cooked through.

SERVES 4

Add meatballs to your favorite spaghetti sauce

PER SERVING
Calories: 143 | Total Fat: 3.8g | Saturated Fat: 2.2g |
Cholesterol: 12.6mg | Sodium: 196.6mg |
Potassium: 787.9mg | Total Carbohydrates: 23.3g |
Dietary Fiber: 9.1g | Sugars: 13.6g | Protein: 7.6g

INDEX

T

Tabbouleh, 111

Tahini, 29, 50, 99

Tomatoes, 16, 19, 39, 41, 55, 59, 83, 93, 103, 107, 111, 113, 119, 121

    diced, 43

    grape, 15, 86, 99

    paste, 89

Tortilla wraps, 65

Tuna, canned, 45, 121

V

Vanilla, 17, 22, 23

Veal, 117

    ground, 101

Vegetables, assorted, 64

Vinegar

    balsamic, 72, 123

    wine, 43

      red, 83

Y

Yogurt, Greek, 17, 45, 79, 81, 91, 109, 112, 125

W

Whole wheat flour, 23

Wine, Marsala, 97

Z

Zucchini, 57, 77, 83, 85, 99

CONVERSION CHART

AN EASY-TO-REFERENCE GUIDE FOR WHEN
YOU TAKE YOUR DIET ABROAD.

VOLUME

¼ teaspoon	1.25 mL
½ teaspoon	2.75 mL
1 teaspoon	5 mL
1 tablespoon	15 mL
¼ cup	60 mL
⅓ cup	80 mL
½ cup	120 mL
⅔ cup	160 mL
¾ cup	180 mL
1 cup	240 mL
1 quart	1 liter
1½ quarts	1.5 liters
2 quarts	2 liters
2½ quarts	2.5 liters
3 quarts	3 liters
4 quarts	4 liters

WEIGHT

1 ounce	30 grams
2 ounces	55 grams
3 ounces	85 grams
4 ounces (¼ pound)	115 grams
8 ounces (½ pound)	225 grams
16 ounces (1 pound)	455 grams
2 pounds	910 grams

LENGTH

⅛ inch	3 mm
¼ inch	6 mm
½ inch	13 mm
¾ inch	19 mm
1 inch	2.5 cm
2 inches	5 cm

TEMPERATURES

Fahrenheit	Celsius
32°	0°
212°	100°
250°	120°
275°	140°
300°	150°
325°	160°
350°	180°
375°	190°
400°	200°
425°	220°
450°	230°
475°	250°
500°	260°

Topix Media Lab
For inquiries, call 646-838-6637

Copyright 2019 Topix Media Lab

Published by Topix Media Lab
14 Wall Street, Suite 4B
New York, NY 10005

Printed in Canada

Note to our readers
The information in this publication should not be substituted for, or used to alter, medical therapy without your doctor's advice. For a specific health problem, consult your physician for guidance.

The information in this publication has been carefully researched, and every reasonable effort has been made to ensure its accuracy. Neither the publication's publisher nor its creators assume any responsibility for any accidents, injuries, losses or other damages that might come from its use. You are solely responsible for taking any and all reasonable and necessary precautions when performing the activities detailed in its pages.

ISBN: 978-1-948174-53-4

CEO Tony Romando

Vice President & Publisher Phil Sexton
Senior Vice President of Sales & New Markets Tom Mifsud
Vice President of Retail Sales & Logistics Linda Greenblatt
Director of Finance Vandana Patel
Manufacturing Director Nancy Puskuldjian
Financial Analyst Matthew Quinn
Brand Marketing & Promotions Assistant Emily McBride

Editor-in-Chief Jeff Ashworth
Creative Director Steven Charny
Photo Director Dave Weiss
Managing Editor Courtney Kerrigan
Senior Editor Tim Baker

Content Editor Juliana Sharaf
Art Director Susan Dazzo
Associate Photo Editor Catherine Armanasco
Associate Editor Trevor Courneen
Copy Editor & Fact Checker Benjamin VanHoose
Designer Kelsey Payne

Co-Founders Bob Lee, Tony Romando

Recipe Development: Isabel Minunni

Indexing by R studio T, NYC
All Photos: Shutterstock

TM21-03

ABOUT THE AUTHOR

ISABEL MINUNNI is a cook, recipe developer, food writer and photographer. She created the popular food blog Bella's Banquet (*bellasbanquet.com*), and has won numerous food and baking competitions, including being named 2014's "Best Italian Chef" by Chef Jeff Mann and Maggiano's Little Italy restaurant chain. One of her favorite cookie recipes was selected from among 4,000 entries for inclusion in *The Barnes & Noble Cookie Bake-Off*. Her numerous TV appearances include both *Today* and *Live with Kelly & Michael*.